KU-769-889

INSIDE WOODY ALLEN

Inside Woody Allen

Selections from the
Comic Strip

Drawn by
Stuart Hample

CORONET BOOKS
Hodder and Stoughton

"Inside Woody Allen" is syndicated in newspapers throughout the United States. It also appears in over sixty foreign countries.

Copyright © 1978 by IWA Enterprises Inc.
Hackenbush Productions Inc.

First published in Great Britain 1978 by Robson Books Limited

Coronet edition 1979

This book is sold subject to the condition that it shall not, by way of trade or otherwise, be lent, re-sold, hired out or otherwise circulated without the publisher's prior consent in any form of binding or cover other than that in which this is published and without a similar condition including this condition being imposed on the subsequent purchaser.

Printed and bound in Great Britain for Hodder and Stoughton Paperbacks, a division of Hodder and Stoughton Ltd., Mill Road, Dunton Green, Sevenoaks, Kent (Editorial Office: 47 Bedford Square, London, WC1 3DP) by Fletcher & Son Ltd, Norwich

ISBN 0 340 24497 6

PHILOSOPHY

PSYCHIATRY

RELATIONS WITH WOMEN

Private Journal - Entry # 3,174.
Why do all the women in my life say I'm a lousy lover?

How can they make a definitive judgment in only 3 minutes?

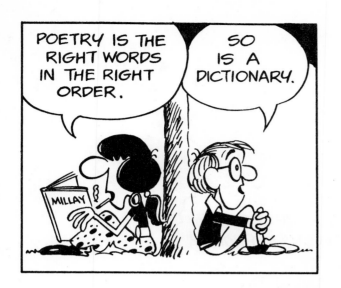

WELL, MAX, I ACTUALLY MET THAT PERFECT WOMAN WE SAW THE OTHER DAY.

AND SHE'S TOO PERFECT TO LIKE YOU, RIGHT? JUST LIKE ALL THE OTHERS.

NOT AT ALL. WE HAVE A DATE ON SATURDAY. OF COURSE I HAD TO LIE FEROCIOUSLY.

YOU'LL NEVER LEARN! SHE'LL DUMP YOU ONCE SHE FINDS OUT THE TRUTH...

BUT SHE **WON'T** FIND OUT THE TRUTH... AS LONG AS I CAN FIND A WAY TO GET FREE RUN OF BUCKINGHAM PALACE ON SATURDAY NIGHT.

4

FAMILY HISTORY & EARLY CHILDHOOD

"I PUT IN 12 YEARS OF RESEARCH AT THE NATIONAL LIBRARY OF INDIAN AFFAIRS...

"...TO UNEARTH THIS HAIR-RAISING STORY FROM THE ALLEN FAMILY HISTORY.

THE ALLENS IN

"WHEN MY GRANDFATHER WAS A BOY, HE WAS KIDNAPPED BY INDIANS FROM THE ALLEN FAMILY HOMESTEAD IN YUMA.

"THE INDIANS RAISED HIM WITH LOVE...

IF YOU LISTEN AFTER 6, THE RATES ARE CHEAPER.

"...BUT IT WAS DIFFICULT BEING THE ONLY ONE IN THE TRIBE WITH RED HAIR AND GLASSES.

HEY, CAN I GO BUFFALO HUNTING WITH YOU GUYS?

YOU, "FOUR-EYES"? HA! HA!

"BUT WHEN MY GREAT-GRANDFATHER LED THE ALLEN CLAN TO RESCUE HIS SON, IT WAS A DISASTER BECAUSE...

"...WHEN INDIANS ATTACK, WAGONS ARE SUPPOSED TO FORM A CIRCLE, LIKE AN "O", BUT HE DIDN'T KNOW THE ALPHABET...

"SO INSTEAD OF AN "O", HE HAD THEM FORM THE LETTER "G"...

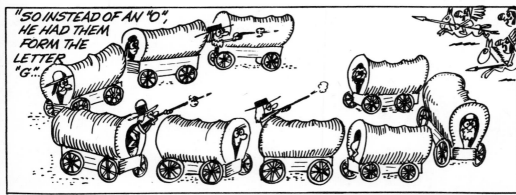

"AND THE INDIANS CAME IN THE OPENING AND MASSACRED THEM!"

"I THINK MY PARENTS WOULD HAVE BEEN PERFECTLY HAPPY IF I HAD BECOME A PHARMACIST...

"OR A SUCCESSFUL DIAMOND SALESMAN.

"BUT I HAD MY OWN DREAM...

"FROM THE TIME I WAS A KID, I ALWAYS WANTED TO BE AN ACTOR, BUT I WAS TOO SHY TO SPEAK UP...

"THEN I READ THAT DEMOSTHENES, THE GREAT GREEK ORATOR, ALSO SPOKE UNCLEARLY WHEN HE WAS YOUNG...

"AND HE CURED HIMSELF BY SPEAKING WITH PEBBLES IN HIS MOUTH.

"SO I TRIED IT...

"...AND I LEARNED TO SPEAK LOUD...

"...BUT I BECAME DEPENDENT ON THE PEBBLES, AND COULD ONLY TALK WHEN THEY WERE IN MY MOUTH.

"THAT WAS O.K. UNTIL I APPEARED IN A SCHOOL PLAY DURING HAY-FEVER SEASON.

"I SNEEZED IN THE FIRST ACT...

"...AND GAVE MR. POE, THE PRINCIPAL, A FRACTURED SKULL."

5

ARTIST/CELEBRITY

6

FORCES OF EVIL

"WHEN I'M DRIVING, I MAKE IT A PRACTICE NEVER TO STOP LATE AT NIGHT FOR HITCH-HIKERS."

"BUT SOMETIMES DETERMINATION IS NOT ENOUGH..."

"ARMED ONLY WITH A SPORTS CAR AND MY FATAL GOOD LOOKS, I SPEED ALONG A SECLUDED ROAD AT NIGHT..."

"A SIX-FOOT-FOUR-INCH HITCH-HIKER WEIGHING 250 LBS. SIGNALS FOR ME TO PICK HIM UP."

"SHREWDLY, I PASS HIM AT 70 M.P.H."

"HE GETS IN."

SPICY FOODS GIVE ME HEARTBURN AND NIGHTMARES.

FOR EXAMPLE: LAST NIGHT, AFTER EATING A PASTRAMI, ONION AND CORNED BEEF ON RYE...

"I DREAM I SAVE A TOWN FROM DESTRUCTION BY A HORDE OF FIERCE VAMPIRE BATS IN METS' UNIFORMS.

"BUT AS THE TOWNFOLK CONGRATULATE ME, THE BATS BEGIN FLYING AROUND.

"I'M TERRIFIED THAT THEY'LL LAND ON ME AND TEAR ME APART.

"BUT SUDDENLY I REALIZE THAT I'M STANDING ON THE RUNWAY OF JFK AIRPORT...

"I BREAK INTO A RUN, GRAB A CAB, AND MAKE MY ESCAPE...

"WHILE THE AIR TRAFFIC CONTROLLER KEEPS THE BATS STACKED OVER THE AIRPORT FOR ANOTHER TWO HOURS...."

AHH...IT'S NOT CROWDED...

HERE'S A NICE SPOT...

"I WAS LYING ON A BEACH WHEN A BULLY THREW SAND IN MY FACE

HERE'S SAND IN YOUR EYE... HA! HA!

I DON'T MIND IT... ANYBODY CAN THROW SAND IN MY FACE AS LONG AS THEY'RE SINCERE.

"BUT WHEN THE SAME BULLY CAME BY FOR 3 STRAIGHT DAYS AND THREW SAND IN MY FACE...

"-I DECIDED TO DO SOMETHING ABOUT IT, BECAUSE IT WAS GETTING RIDICULOUS. SO I TOOK DANCING LESSONS.

Learn to DANCE
TANGO SALSA MAMBO
1 FLITE UP
WA

"TRUE, THAT WOULDN'T HELP ME DEFEND MYSELF, BUT AT LEAST I COULD PROVIDE A MOVING TARGET.

"2 WEEKS LATER, I'M LYING ON THE BEACH, AND AS HE'S ABOUT TO THROW SAND IN MY FACE...

"I BREAK OUT INTO A TANGO.

IT TOOK HIM SO COMPLETELY OFF GUARD, HE DROPPED HIS SAND AND STARTED TO TANGO ALONG WITH ME, BUT...

"WHILE I WAS TRYING TO FIGURE OUT MY NEXT MOVE, WE WERE BOTH ARRESTED BY THE VICE SQUAD FOR DANCING IN A PUBLIC PLACE WITHOUT GIRLS"

POLICE